35858

LIKE
NOTHING
AT ALL

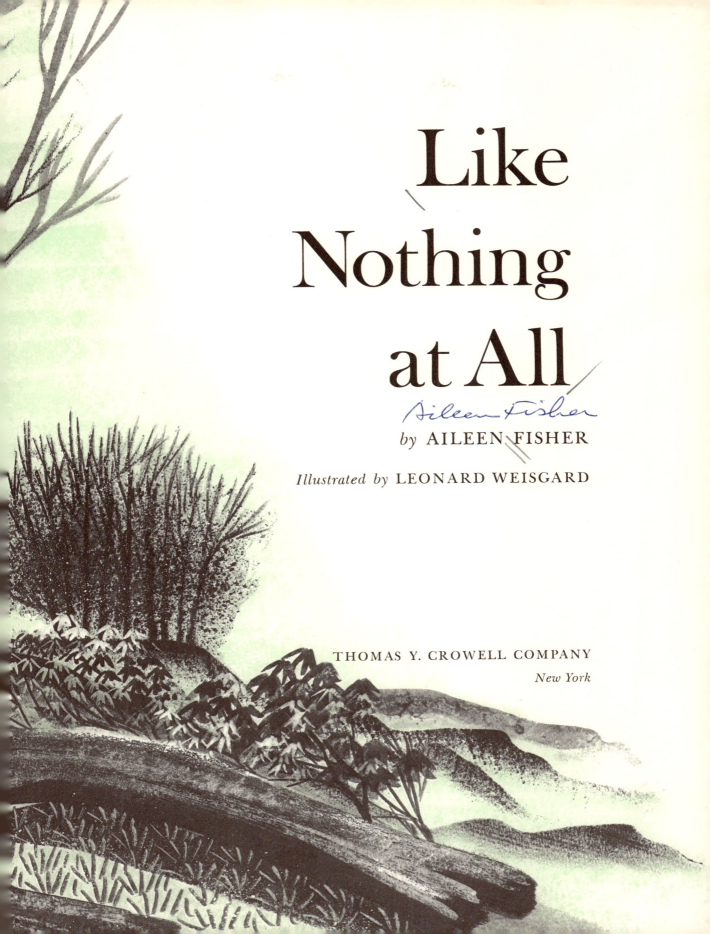

Like
Nothing
at All

Aileen Fisher

by AILEEN FISHER

Illustrated by LEONARD WEISGARD

THOMAS Y. CROWELL COMPANY
New York

To my mother

When I went walking
in early spring,
do you know what I saw?

A hump of a thing—
a hump of
a bump of
a clump of a thing,
sort of tannish
and sort of brownish
under a bush
and all slumped-downish,
like grass or weeds
the color of hay
faded by winter
that moved away,
not the waking-up green
of a gay spring day,
nor the waking-up color
of April or May.

Of course, in spring
there's a lot to see:
a butterfly
and a bumblebee,
bright buds clinging
to every tree,
wildflowers
springing up eagerly...
and robins singing
inside of me!

I saw what neither
was big nor small.
It looked like grass
left over from fall,
hunchy, bunchy,
and halfway tall.

But mostly it looked
like Nothing at All.

Like nothing at all!

Then what do you think?
When I walked by
it jumped in a wink.
It leaped through the sky!
And off it went bouncing,
flouncing,
hopping,
straight for the woods
and never stopping
until it was gone
in the blink of an eye.
In the blink of an eye!

And I jumped, too,
because you-know-why:
I wasn't expecting a Jump
near by,
a whisk of a
frisk of a
Jump near by.

Do you know
what it was?

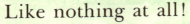

A COTTONTAIL RABBIT!

It looked like nothing
but weeds or hay
until it got frightened
and bounced away
that early spring day
before it was April,
before it was May.

In summer I walked
in an aspen wood
where the grass was green
and the ferns smelled good.

Do you know what I saw
when I stopped and stood?

I stood where the sun
came through the spaces
between the leaves
like freckles on faces,
like speckles
and fleckles
of dancing light
till the ferns were dappled,
and left and right
the dried old leaves
on the woodsy ground
were speckled with sun
when I looked around. . . .

When I looked around
I was hoping to see
something that looked
like Nothing to me:
something possibly
two feet tall
but hard to see
when cuddled-up small
with his knees
tucked under his chin, and all.

He wouldn't blink
so much as an eye
or kink an ear
when a step went by . . .
he'd lie in his coat
of reddish-brown
with spots on his back
from tail to crown
like fleckles of sun
when the sun shone down. . . .

When the sun shone down
on the aspen wood,
I looked
and looked
but I wasn't much good.
I only saw Nothing
from where I stood,
only Nothing
from where I stood.

I stared,
and *stared*.
And then...I saw it!
So like Nothing
I never could draw it,
so like Nothing
I hardly could spy it
under the aspens,
dappled and quiet.

Do you know what I saw?

A SPOTTED FAWN!

You scarcely can tell
when you look at one
which speckles are *fawn*
and which are *sun*.

Walking in fall
when the sky was hazy
and hills were sleepy
and pines were lazy,
I hardly could feel
a whiff of breeze
but bright leaves did . . .
on the aspen trees,
golden-yellow before my eyes
like hovery thousands
of butterflies,
like thousands and thousands
of butterflies.

I walked past a hill
and down a valley:
fall is the time
to dream and dally.

I watched the sun
on the river glisten:
fall is the time
to look and listen.

I came to some firs
and skirted under:
fall is the time
to watch and wonder.

I thought there was nothing
but woods ahead
with splashes of brown
and dashes of red
and flashes of sun,
or shade instead,
and a tree fallen down
on a pine-needle bed,

Till, suddenly . . . whoosh!
in a noisy flurry,
with a whirr,
all astir,
in a frightful hurry
something rose up
before my face
and flew away
through the trees
some place!

To think I had stepped
on something . . . nearly!
Mottled
and spotted
and marked so queerly,
it looked like merely
Nothing at All
on the ground in fall.

Like nothing at all.

What do you think it was?

A GROUSE!

Some birds *show*,
but others are clever
at looking like Nothing
forever and ever.

I walked in winter
where pines wore mittens,
fluffy and white
and soft as kittens,
where every bush
wore a white wool cap
with an ear-muff flap,
and an ermine wrap,
and the pond
had eiderdown on its lap.

And hills were billows
of puffed-up pillows,
and piping showed
on the twigs of willows.

I thought, "Oh, oh,
where the wild folk go
through a world of snow
their colors will show."

I saw some tracks
where a mouse had traveled
and left the hem of the snow
unraveled.

I saw a hole
where the tracks dove down
to grass that was yellow
and seeds that were brown
and roots that were sweet
for a mouse to eat.

When I turned to go
through the snowy meadow,
a quick white streak
with a quick gray shadow
flashed in a whiff
through the white ahead.
Was it real?
Was it live?
Was it wind, instead?

Something little
and something white
whirled through the snow
and swirled from sight.

Telltale tracks
bigger than a mouse's,
smaller than a rabbit's,
smaller than a grouse's
lay on the snow,
but I never did see
really-and-truly as it should be
what looked like a whisk
of Nothing to me.

What do you think it was?

A WEASEL!

A weasel in summer
is buffy and brown,
but he's white as snow
when the snow comes down,
except for a flick
of inky black
on the tippermost tip
of his tail in back.

I got thinking,
I got blinking,
I got thinking of clothes I wear:
bright clothes,
light clothes,
never-out-of-sight clothes
keep me showing, everywhere.
Coming or going,
sunning or snowing,
everybody's knowing
I am there!

So you know what I did?

I thought of a game
that hasn't a name,
and played it in April
when April came.
I wasn't a fawn
or weasel
or rabbit
or grouse
with a looking-like-nothing habit,
but just the same . . .

I dug out my Mother's
old green smock
and my Dad's brown hat
like an old brown rock,

I splotched the smock
with yellow for sun
and purple for shade,
and I sat for fun
in the lilac clump
like a hump
like a bump
all ready to jump.

My Mother didn't see me
when she went by.

My brother didn't see me,
and you know *why*.

My sister didn't see me.
Neither would you!

My Father didn't see me
when he passed, too.

I looked like Nothing,
nothing at all,
nothing too big,
nothing too small,
I looked as hidden
as Nothings do . . .

until I wiggled

and the brown hat jiggled

and the green smock wriggled

and I jumped and giggled

and called, "YOO-HOO!"

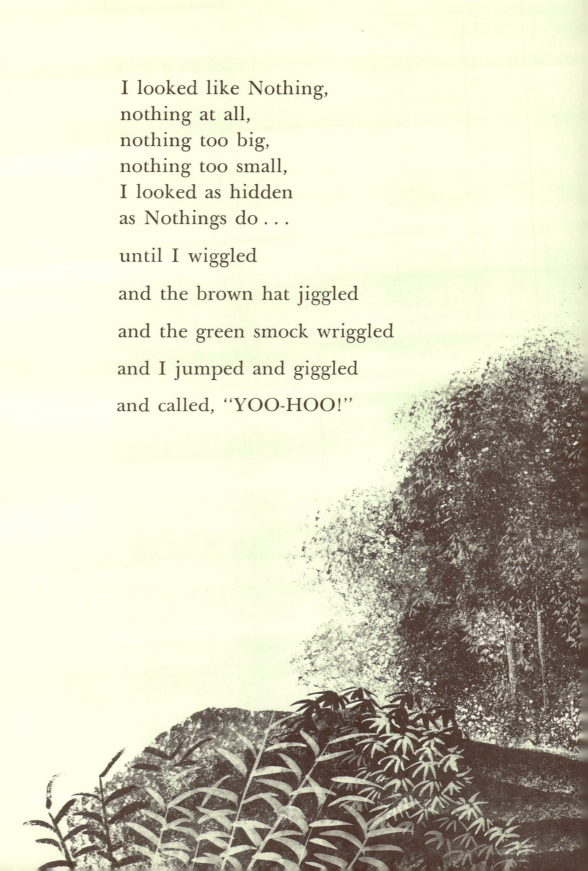

ABOUT THE AUTHOR

AILEEN FISHER grew up on a farm in Michigan
where she first became aware of the animals
she writes of with joy and perception and
the beauty and fun of the changing seasons.

Miss Fisher now lives on a two-hundred-
acre ranch near Boulder, Colorado. From the
window of her cabin, which she helped build,
she has a magnificent view of hills and
mountains. She delights in hiking and in
fashioning fantastic creatures from pieces
of wood she finds along the way.

ABOUT THE ILLUSTRATOR

LEONARD WEISGARD has had a wide variety of
art experience. He has designed covers
for *The New Yorker* magazine and labels for ham,
painted eyes on mannequins and murals
for Macy's, and illustrated and designed
innumerable books for children. His special
interests, other than children and
their books, are people, animals, the theater
in all its forms, and Americana.

Mr. Weisgard is a resident of Connecticut.
He was born in New Haven and now lives
in Roxbury with his wife and three children.
Mr. Weisgard is Chairman of the Roxbury Board of Education.